MARGRET REY

Curious George Flies a Kite

Pictures by
H. A. REY

HOUGHTON MIFFLIN COMPANY BOSTON

Library of Congress Catalog Card Number: 58-8163
ISBN: 0-395-16965-8 (rnf.)
ISBN: 0-395-25937-1 (pbk.)

Printed in the U.S.A.

WOZ   **Forty Fifth Printing**

This is George.

He lives in the house
of the man with the yellow hat.

George is a little monkey,
and all monkeys are curious.

But no monkey
is as curious as George.

That is why his name is
Curious George.

"I have to go out now,"
said the man with the yellow hat.
"Be a good little monkey
till I come back.
Have fun and play
with your new ball,
but do not be too curious."
And the man went out.

It was
a lot of fun
for George
to play with
his big new ball.
   The ball
went up,
and George
went up,

and the ball
went down,
and George
went down.

George could
do a lot of tricks
with his ball too.
This was one
of the tricks.
He could get up
on the ball like this.

Or do it this way,
with his head down.

This was
another trick
George could do.
He could hold
the ball on his head,
like this.

Look—no hands.
What a good trick!
But—but where did the ball go?

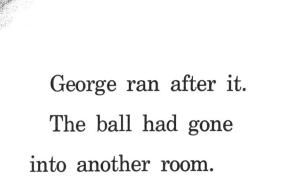

George ran after it.

The ball had gone

into another room.

There was
a big window
in the room.

George liked to look
out of that window.

He could see
a lot from there.

He let the ball go
and looked out.

George
could see
Bill on his bike
and the lake
with a boat
on it.

George
could see
a big house
in a little garden
and a little house
in a big garden.

The big house
was the house
where Bill lived.

But who lived

in the little house?

George was curious.

Who could live in a house

that was so little?

George had to find out,
so he went to the big garden.
The garden had a high wall,
but not too high
for a monkey.
George got up on the wall.

All he had to do now
was jump down—
so George jumped down
into the big garden.

Now he could take a good look
at the little house.

And what did he see?

A big white bunny
and a lot of little bunnies.

George looked and looked and looked.

Bunnies were something new to him.

How funny they were!

The big bunny

was Mother Bunny.

She was as big as George.

But the little bunnies were so little

that George could hold

one of them in his hand,

and that is what he wanted to do.

How could he get a bunny
out of the house?

A house must have a door
to get in and to get out.

But where was the door
to the bunny house?

Oh—there it was!

George put his hand in
and took out
a baby bunny.

What fun it was
to hold a baby bunny!
And the bunny did not mind.
It sat in his hand,
one ear up and one ear down
and looked at George,
and George looked back at it.

Now he and the bunny
could play in the garden.

They could play a game.

They could play Get the Bunny.

George would let the bunny hop away,
and then he would run after it
and get it back.

George put the bunny down.

Then he looked away.

One—two—run!

The bunny was off like a shot.

George did not look.

Now he had to wait a little.

One—two—three—four—he waited.

Then George looked up.
Where was the bunny?
He could not see it.
Where was it?
Where had it gone?

George looked for it here,
and he looked for it there.
He could not find it.

Where was the bunny?

It could not get

out of the garden.

It could not get up the wall

the way George could.

It could not fly away.

It had to be here—

but it was not.

The bunny was gone,

and all the fun

was gone too.

George sat down.

He had been a bad little monkey.

Why was he so curious?

Why did he let the bunny go?

Now he could not put it

back into the bunny house

where it could be

with Mother Bunny.

Bad monkey.

Mother Bunny—George looked up.

Why, that was it!

Mother Bunny could help him!

George got up.

He had to have some string.

Maybe there was some in the garden.

Yes, there was a string
and a good one too.

George took the string
and went back
to the bunny house.

Mother Bunny

was at the door.

George let her out

and put the string on her.

And Mother Bunny knew what to do.

Away she went
with her head down
and her ears up.

All George could do was
hold the string
and run after her.

And then Mother Bunny sat down.

She saw something,

and George saw it too.

Something white

that looked like a tail,

like the tail of the baby bunny.

And that is what it was!

But where was the rest of the bunny?

It was down in a hole.

A bunny likes to dig a hole
and then go down and live in it.

But this bunny was too little
to live in a hole.

It should live in a bunny house.

So George got hold
of the little white tail
and pulled the baby bunny out.

Then they all ran back
to the bunny house.

George did not have to put a string
on the baby bunny.

It ran after its mother
all the way home.

George took the string
off Mother Bunny
and helped them back
into the house.

Then Mother Bunny,
and all the little ones
lay down to sleep.

George looked at them.

It was good to see the baby bunny
back where it should be.

And now George would go
back to where he should be.

When he came to the wall,
he could see something funny
in back of it.

George got up on the wall
to find out what it was.

He saw
a long string
on a long stick.
A fat man
had the long stick
in his hand.
What could the man do
with a stick that long?
George was curious.

The fat man was

on his way to the lake,

and soon George was

on his way to the lake too.

The man took a hook

out of his box,

put it on a string

and then put something on the hook.

Then the man let the string
down into the water
and waited.

Now George knew!

The string on the stick
was to fish with.

When the man pulled the string
out of the water,
there was a big fish on the hook.
George saw the man
pull one fish after another
out of the lake,
till he had
all the fish
he wanted.

What fun

it must be to fish!

George wanted to fish too.

He had his string.

All he needed was a stick,

and he knew where to get that.

George ran home as fast as he could.

In the kitchen
he took the mop
off the kitchen wall.

The mop would make
a good stick.

Now George had the string and the stick.

He was all set to fish.

Or was he?

Not yet.

George had to have a hook

and on the hook something

that fish like to eat.

Fish would like cake,

and George knew where to find some.

But where could he get a hook?

Why—there was a hook

for the mop on the kitchen wall!

It would have

to come out.

With the hook

on the string

and the string

on the stick

and the cake

in the box

in his hand,

George went back

to the lake.

George sat down,

put some cake on the hook,

and let the line down into the water.

Now he had to wait,

just as the man had waited.

George was curious.

The fish were curious too.
All kinds of fish came
to look at the line,
big fish and little fish,
fat fish and thin fish,
red fish and yellow fish
and blue fish.

One of them was near the hook.
The cake was just what he wanted.

George sat and waited.

Then the line shook.

There must be a fish on the hook.

George pulled the line up.

The cake was gone,

but no fish was on the hook.

Too bad!

George put more cake on the hook.

Maybe this time

he would get a fish.

But no!

The fish just took the cake

off the hook

and went away.

Well, if George
could not get the fish,
the fish would not get the cake.

George would eat it.

He liked cake too.

He would find another way
to get a fish.

George looked into the water.

That big red one there

with the long tail!

It was so near,

maybe he could get it

with his hands.

George got down

as low as he could,

and put out his hand.

SPLASH!

Into the lake he went!

The water was cold and wet
and George was cold and wet too.
This was no fun at all.

When he came out of the water,

Bill was there with his kite.

"My, you are wet!" Bill said.

"I saw you fall in,

so I came to help you get out.

Too bad you did not get a fish!

But it is good the fish

did not get you."

"Now I can show you how high
my kite can fly," Bill went on.

Bill put his bike up near a tree
and then they ran off.

There was a lot of wind that day,
and that was just what they needed.
The wind took the kite up fast.
George was too little
to hold it in this wind.

A kite that big
could fly away with him.
So Bill had to hold it.
George saw the kite
go up and up and up.
What fun it was to fly a kite!

They let the kite fly
for a long time
till Bill said,

"I will get the kite down now.

I must go home
and you should too."

But when Bill pulled the string in,
the kite got into the top
of a high tree.

Bill could not get it down.

"Oh, my fine new kite!

I can not let go of it.

I must have it back,"
Bill said.

"But the tree

is too high for me."

But no tree
was too high for George.
He went up to the top
in no time.

Then, little by little,
he got the string
out of the tree.

Down he came
with the kite
and gave it back
to Bill.

"Thank you, George, thanks a lot,"
Bill said. "I am so happy
to have the kite back.

Now you may have
a ride home on my bike.

I will run back to the lake
and get it.

You wait here for me
with the kite,
but do not let it fly away."

George looked at the kite.

Then he took the string in his hand.

He knew he could not fly the kite
in this wind,
but maybe he could let it
go up just a little bit.

George was curious.

He let the string go a little,
and then a little more,
and then a little more,
and then a little more.

When Bill came back,
there was no kite
and there was no George.
"George!" he called.
"Where are you?"

Then he looked up.

There they were,

way up in the sky!

Bill had to get help fast.

He would go to the man

with the yellow hat.

The man would know

what to do.

"George is not here,"
said the man with the yellow hat
when Bill came.

"Have you seen him?"

"George and my kite
are up in the sky
near the lake," Bill shouted.

"I came to . . ."

But the man did not wait
to hear any more.

He ran to his car and jumped in.

"I will get him back," he said.

"I must get George back."

All this time

the wind took the kite up

and George with it.

It was fun

to fly about in the sky.

But when George looked down,

the fun was gone.

He was up so high

that all the big houses

looked as little as bunny houses.

George did not like it a bit.

He wanted to get down, but how?

Not even a monkey

can jump from the sky.

George was scared.

What if he never got back?

Maybe he would fly

on and on and on.

Oh, he would never, never

be so curious again,

if just this one time

he could find a way to get home.

Hummmmm—hummmmm.

What was that?

George could hear something,
and then he saw something
fly in the sky just like a kite.

It was a helicopter,

and in the helicopter,

hurrah,

was the man with the yellow hat!

Down from
the helicopter
came a long line.
George got hold of it,
and the man with the yellow hat
pulled him up.
George held on to the kite,
for he had to give it back to Bill.

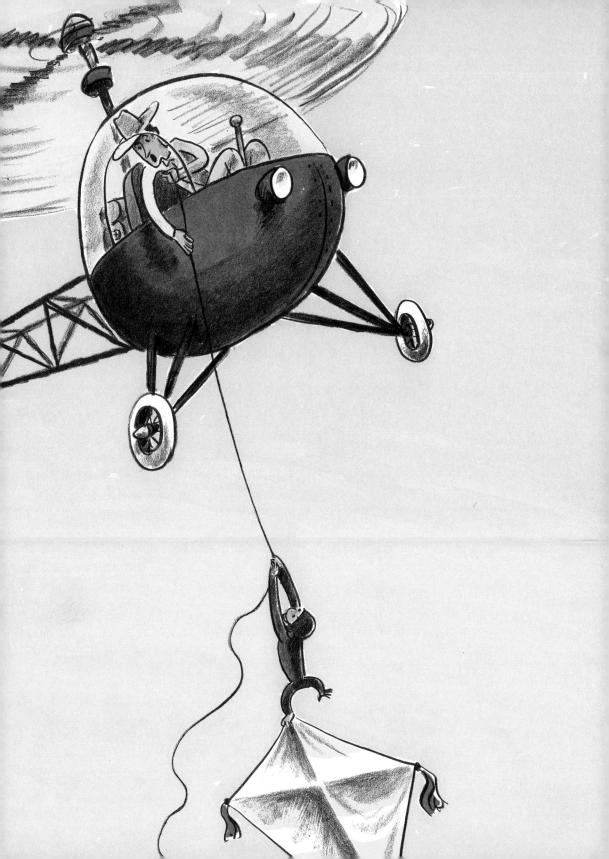

"I am so happy
to have you back, George,"
said the man with the yellow hat.

"I was scared,
and you must have been scared too.

I know you will not want
to fly a kite again
for a long, long time.

You must give it back to Bill
when we get home."

72

"Hurrah!" Bill shouted
when George came
to give him the kite.
"George is back,
and my kite is back too!"

And then Bill
took George by the hand
and went with him
into the little garden,

and from the little garden
into the big garden,
where the bunny house was.

"Here is one of my baby bunnies,"
Bill said.

"Take it, it is for you!"

A baby bunny for George!

George took it in his hands

and held it way up.

It was HIS bunny now.

He could take it home with him.

And that is

what he

did.

Babies are such a nice way to start people.

—DON HEROLD

A
MOTHER'S
J O U R N A L

RUNNING PRESS
PHILADELPHIA · LONDON

The biggest problem facing a pregnant woman is not nausea or fatigue or her wardrobe—it's free advice. I learned very quickly to agree with everyone. I would smile and say, "Of course, you are so right. What an excellent idea!" Then I would go on doing whatever I knew to be right for my baby. Everyone was happy.

—SOPHIA LOREN

The street's abloom with pregnant women. They stand next to me in elevators. I see them on movie lines, getting out of taxicabs, choosing fruit and vegetables . . . Were they here before I was pregnant? Will they all disappear when I give birth? After that, will I only notice new mothers and new babies?

—PHYLLIS CHESLER

Such solicitous care I have never had. Chairs pulled out for me, things picked up for me, milk offered me, an arm offered for high steps . . . At first it bothered me; now I think it rather a relief—sometimes very funny and sometimes very nice.

—ANNE MORROW LINDBERGH

Ah, to be skinny herself! To sleep on her flat stomach, walk lightly again on the balls of her feet.

—DORIS BETTS

You are entirely engrossed in your own body and the life it holds. It is as if you were in the grip of a powerful force; as if a wave had lifted you above and beyond everyone else. In this way there is always a part of a pregnant woman that is unreachable and is reserved for the future—her baby.

—SOPHIA LOREN

And there he was—a red-faced, black-haired, frowning baby . . . a real person with hands and feet and a real face. They whisked him away. Something was real and alive inside that blue blanket I had bought so casually in Macy's. A real creature, all mine.

—DOROTHY EVSLIN

In the reveries of her pregnancy, he was a mental image with infinite possibilities; and the mother enjoyed her future maternity in thought; now he is a tiny, finite individual, and he is there in reality—dependent, delicate, demanding.

—SIMONE DE BEAUVOIR

The commonest fallacy among women is that simply having children makes one a mother—which is as absurd as believing that having a piano makes one a musician.

—SYDNEY J. HARRIS

I cannot stop marvelling at her perfect formation, her peaceful sleeping face, and her shock of black hair. I feel awkward and uncomfortable about handling her, but I am learning.

—SIMONE BLOOM

In the sheltered simplicity of the first days after a baby is born, one sees again the magical closed circle, the miraculous sense of two people existing only for each other.

—ANNE MORROW LINDBERGH

Why was it that so many women artists who had renounced having children could then paint nothing but mothers and children?

—ERICA JONG

Every mother I know has suddenly been elevated to heroine in my mind. I feel a special closeness toward my own mother, even though she is literally at the other end of the world.

—SIMONE BLOOM

*There is an amazed curiosity in every young mother. It is strangely
miraculous to see and to hold a living being formed within oneself and
issued forth from oneself.*

—SIMONE DE BEAUVOIR

Discovering an ability to love uncritically and totally has been exhilarating. It's the sort of love that calls upon my whole being, bringing all of my potential to life.

—RONNIE FRIEDLAND

I actually remember feeling delight, at two o'clock in the morning, when the baby woke for his feed, because I so longed to have another look at him.

—MARGARET DRABBLE

I often feel a spiritual communion with all the other mothers who are feeding their babies in the still of the night. Having a baby makes me feel a general closeness with humanity.

—SIMONE BLOOM

Enchanting is that baby-laugh, all dimples
and glitter—so strangely arch and innocent!

—MARGARET FULLER OSSOLI

During the first six months, the baby has the rudiments of a love language available to him. There is the language of the embrace, the language of the eyes, the language of the smile, vocal communications of pleasure and distress. It is the essential vocabulary of love before we can speak of love.

—SELMA FRAIBERG

Once Eleza was doing more than merely screaming or sleeping, I wanted to talk endlessly about our adorable and clever little petunia blossom. Who else was as interested in her as I? Who else but my husband could appreciate the subtle changes that go unobserved by all others?

—CAROL KORT

Jennie smiles for the first time—a gentle parting of her lips into a contented, happy crinkle, and we are filled with delight and excitement. We get out her baby book and make the first notation.

—SIMONE BLOOM

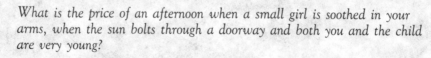

What is the price of an afternoon when a small girl is soothed in your arms, when the sun bolts through a doorway and both you and the child are very young?

—DOROTHY EVSLIN

Motherhood brings as much joy as ever, but it still brings boredom, exhaustion, and sorrow too. Nothing else ever will make you as happy or as sad, as proud or as tired, for nothing is quite as hard as helping a person develop his own individuality—especially while you struggle to keep your own.

—MARGUERITE KELLY and ELIA PARSONS

When they are a few months old, they lie and look around and wave and smile and undergo a constant gentle agitation, as though they were sea anemones, gently waving in some other element, delicately responding to currents we cannot feel.

—MARGARET DRABBLE

I am amazed (and secretly delighted) at how many people stop me to have a look at my baby. Motherhood seems to break all social barriers as conversations with strangers of all ages and backgrounds evolve.

—SIMONE BLOOM

List the different activities a mother performs in the course of any one day with her child, and their range—from nose-wiping to rocking, from offering the breast to scolding—will be truly astounding.

—RUDOLPH SCHAFFER

Parenthood remains the greatest single preserve of the amateur.

—ALVIN TOFFLER

This sense of connection with other mothers—both old and young—is a wonderful addition to my life. Motherhood has enabled me to connect with a whole new spectrum of people—those who have families.

—RONNIE FRIEDLAND

Being a mother enables one to influence the future.

—JANE SELLMAN

Learning how to be a mother is not a matter of adopting a certain set of attitudes, but of expressing one's own personality in the task of responding flexibly to the child's needs.

—SHEILA KITZINGER

I fold the drab maternity pants with the frayed elastic waistband and place them back in the box. Then I put the box away—for now.

—CAROL KORT

A child of one can be taught not to do certain things such as touch a hot stove, turn on the gas, pull lamps off their tables by their cords, or wake Mommy before noon.

—JOAN RIVERS

I discovered when I had a child of my own that I had become a biased observer of small children. Instead of looking at them with affection but nonpartisan eyes, I saw each of them as older or younger, bigger or smaller, more or less graceful, intelligent, or skilled than my own child.

—MARGARET MEAD

. . . Giving advice comes naturally to mothers. Advice is in the genes along with blue eyes and red hair.

—LOIS WYSE

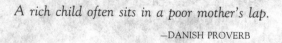

A rich child often sits in a poor mother's lap.

—DANISH PROVERB

*A mother understands
what a child does not say.*
—JEWISH PROVERB

*A mother is not a person to lean on
but a person to make leaning unnecessary.*

—DOROTHY CANFIELD FISHER

It's easy to complain about children. But when we want to express our joy, our love, the words elude us. The feelings are almost so sacred they defy speech.

—JOAN McINTOSH

Being a mother, as far as I can tell, is a constantly evolving process of adapting to the needs of your child while also changing and growing as a person in your own right.

—DEBORAH INSEL

Before I got married I had six theories about bringing up children; now I have six children, and no theories.

—LORD ROCHESTER

Some are kissing mothers and some are scolding mothers, but it is love just the same, and most mothers kiss and scold together.

—PEARL S. BUCK

The phrase "working mother" is redundant.

—JANE SELLMAN

Mothering should involve both taking care of someone who is dependent and at the same time supporting that person in his or her efforts to become independent.

—SIGNE HAMMER

To talk to a child, to fascinate him, is much more difficult than to win an electoral victory. But it is more rewarding.

—COLETTE

The surface of a table can be cluttered and breakable in exact proportion to the age of the children who pass it by.

—DOROTHY EVSLIN

Govern a family as you would cook small fish—very gently.

—CHINESE PROVERB

It is difficult to give children a sense of security unless you have it yourself. If you have it, they catch it from you.

—WILLIAM C. MENNINGER, M.D.

For the hand that rocks the cradle is the hand that rules the world.

—WILLIAM ROSS WALLACE

If evolution really works,
how come mothers have only two hands?

—ED DUSSAULT

All of these concepts seemed easy for her to grasp, which surprised me. Where had I been when she was tooling up her brain?

—PHYLLIS THEROUX

When you are dealing with a child, keep all your wits about you, and sit on the floor.

—AUSTIN O'MALLEY

*There was never a child so lovely but his mother
was glad to get him asleep.*

—RALPH WALDO EMERSON

As I picked her up and peeled off the warm damp layers, I had this strange feeling of female communion. We two girls were safe in the nursery, away from the noisy male warren.

—DOROTHY EVSLIN

The parents exist to teach the child, but also they must learn what the child has to teach them; and the child has a very great deal to teach them.

—ARNOLD BENNETT

When you are a mother, you are never really alone in your thoughts. You are connected to your child and to all those who touch your lives. A mother always has to think twice, once for herself and once for her child.

—SOPHIA LOREN

One child would not interfere very much with our work. One child could always be put to bed in a bureau drawer. It was having two children that really changed life.

—MARGARET MEAD

*Now, as always, the most automated appliance
in a household is the mother.*

—BEVERLY JONES

In motherhood, there's so much to learn, so much to give, and although the learning gets less with each succeeding child, the giving never does.

—MARGUERITE KELLY and ELIA PARSONS

"Look!" my mother and my aunts would cry out to each baby in turn as it shook a rattle, stood up, peed in a pot, took the cover off a box and fitted it on again: *"Look"*—in joyous amazement, as if such a thing had never been seen before—*"what the baby can do!"*

—DOROTHY DINNERSTEIN

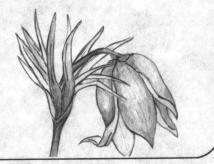

The third baby is the easiest one to have . . . You know, for instance, how you're going to look in a maternity dress about the seventh month, and you know how to release the footbrake on a baby carriage without fumbling amateurishly, and you know how to tie your shoes before and do knee-chests after, and while you're not exactly casual, you're a little offhand about the whole thing.

—SHIRLEY JACKSON

My daughters enlighten me about myself. Their presence acts as a constant, ever-changing reflection of me as well as a source of feedback, as I see myself mirrored in their mannerisms, attitudes, and relationships.

—ELLEN A. ROSEN

The mother-child relationship is paradoxical and, in a sense, tragic. It requires the most intense love on the mother's side, yet this very love must help the child grow away from the mother, and to become fully independent.

—ERICH FROMM

Every child needs a lap.

—BENJAMIN WEININGER
and HENRY RABIN

Sentimental people keep insisting that women go on to have a third baby because they love babies, and cynical people seem to maintain that a woman with two healthy, active children around the house will do anything for ten quiet days in the hospital.

—SHIRLEY JACKSON

*The events of childhood do not pass, but
repeat themselves like seasons of the year.*

—ELEANOR FARJEON

A suburban mother's role is to deliver children obstetrically once, and by car forever after.

—PETER DE VRIES

Children need love, especially when they do not deserve it.

—HAROLD S. HULBERT

Any adult who spends even fifteen minutes with a child outdoors finds himself drawn back to his own childhood, like Alice falling down the rabbit hole.

—SHARON MacLATCHIE

If you bend over backwards for your children,
you will eventually lose your balance.

—JOHN ROSEMOND

An unbreakable toy is good for breaking other toys.

—JOHN PEERS

You cannot teach a child to take care of himself unless you will let him try to take care of himself. He will make mistakes; and out of these mistakes will come his wisdom.

—FRANCIS BACON

The quickest way for a parent to get a child's attention is to sit down and look comfortable.

—LANE OLINGHOUSE

I suppose there must be in every mother's life the inevitable moment when she has to take two small children shopping in one big store.

—SHIRLEY JACKSON

Judicious mothers will always keep in mind that they are the first book read, and the last put aside, in every child's library.

—C. LENOX REMOND

We say "I love you" to our children, but it's not enough. Maybe that's why mothers hug and hold and rock and kiss and pat.

—JOAN McINTOSH

For years, my husband and I have advocated separate vacations. But the kids keep finding us.

—ERMA BOMBECK

In a child's lunch box, a mother's thoughts.

—JAPANESE PROVERB

Keeping house is like threading beads on a string
with no knot at the end.

—ANONYMOUS

My children would not like me to have a face-lift. They say, "Oh, Mommy, don't change—you are so beautiful, and you will always be so beautiful." So, I feel very well in my skin.

—SOPHIA LOREN

There is so much to teach, and the time goes so fast.

—ERMA BOMBECK

*Children are likely to live up to
what you believe of them.*

—LADY BIRD JOHNSON

Mother has an uncanny way of thinking that if she doesn't tell us about something, we will never find out, that she is our only source of knowledge.

—NANCY FRIDAY

When I stopped seeing my mother with the eyes of a child, I saw the woman who helped me give birth to myself.

—NANCY FRIDAY

There are three ways to get something done: do it yourself, hire someone, or forbid your kids to do it.

—MONTA CRANE

It will be gone before you know it. The fingerprints on the wall appear higher and higher. Then suddenly they disappear.

—DOROTHY EVSLIN

Insanity is hereditary—
you get it from your children.

—SAM LEVINSON

I think it must somewhere be written, that the virtues of mothers shall be visited on their children. . . .

—CHARLES DICKENS

. . . *The hardest of all is learning to be a well of affection and not a fountain, to show them that we love them, not when we feel like it, but when they do.*

*There's nothing wrong with teenagers
that reasoning with them won't aggravate.*

—ANONYMOUS

No man can ever appreciate the debt he owes his mother, but sometimes
a little thing may come up to set him thinking.

—EDWIN ARLINGTON ROBINSON

No matter how old a mother is, she watches her middle-aged children for signs of improvement.

—FLORIDA SCOTT-MAXWELL

I've become a mother. That's why women grow up and men don't.

—KATHLEEN CLEAVER

For me, motherhood has been the one true, great, and wholly successful romance. It is the only love I have known that is expansive and that could have stretched to contain with equal passion more than one object. . . .

—IRMA KURTZ

My mother had a great deal of trouble with me,
but I think she enjoyed it.

—MARK TWAIN (SAMUEL L. CLEMENS)